Looking At Life

Piece By Piece

by Kristen Kemper

LOOKING AT LIFE PIECE BY PIECE

by Kristen Kemper

Copyright © 1996 Educational Ministries, Inc.

ISBN 1-57438-004-4

Educational Ministries, Inc.

165 Plaza Drive

Prescott, AZ 86303

800-221-0910

TABLE OF CONTENTS

‖ntroduction

Today's youth face more influences and choices than ever. They need guidance and support in the process of establishing their individual identities and choosing what is important to their lives. As facilitator of a youth group, you have the opportunity to help youth find this support in the church. The programs included in <u>Looking At Life Piece by Piece</u> will challenge youth to explore their beliefs and feelings, while giving them an opportunity to gain insights from the reflections and opinions of the other participants. While several of the 24 programs are offered for use during specific seasons or holidays, the majority cover issues and topics that are of everyday concern to youth. The programs are not necessarily intended to be presented in the order in which they appear. They should be developed and presented when you believe they would be most beneficial in meeting the needs of your group.

Each program includes a section called **In Preparation** which offers material for the facilitator to ponder in preparing for the program. You should plan on spending several hours in preparation for each program. Read through the material of the selected program, study and review it. Try some of the suggested activities yourself. As you do, think of other appropriate activities, questions and scriptures that you might add to the program. Throughout the process of preparation you should always keep in mind, and be sensitive to, the individuals in your group and how they may be impacted by the particular topic to be discussed.

A variety of techniques are suggested in each of the programs to keep the youth actively involved in exploring the themes. It is through discussion, however, that the youth will learn the most. Thus, the ultimate goal of all the activities is to create opportunities for meaningful dialogue. Such dynamic interaction will only take place if a community of acceptance is created in which participants do not fear being rejected. To ensure an atmosphere of trust, stress to participants the importance of never repeating anything that is said during a program outside of the youth group. Also let the participants know that putting down others, or their ideas and opinions, will not be tolerated. Some rules should also be followed to ensure effective discussions. First, everyone should be allowed to talk but no one should be forced to do so. Second, no one should be allowed to dominate the conversation. Finally, remember that your role as facilitator is to guide the conversation and keep it flowing, not to lecture, preach or force your opinions on others. Respect the ideas and opinions of the youth and they in turn will respect yours.

Levels Of Trust

Trust is the key ingredient in a meaningful relationship. Believing in others is a key concept in the Christian faith. Yet trust is a risk and therefore often difficult, particularly in a society in which public officials and televangelists are often caught in illegal acts. In this program youth will explore their relationships and hopefully come to understand better the role trust plays in them. The discussion and activities will also give them a better understanding of what it means to be trustworthy.

In Preparation

As facilitator of the group, you should spend some time thinking about the trust relationships in which you are involved. Make a list of these and rate the level of trust of each, just as you will ask the youth to. It is also important that you take the time to evaluate the degree of trust that is present within the youth group. Do members feel secure enough to open up and express their true thoughts and feelings? If you keep this question in the back of your mind during this session, the discussions could be very revealing

Opening The Program

Open the session by inviting the youth to make individual lists of their trust relationships. Their lists might include family members (parents, grandparents, siblings, cousins, aunts and uncles), friends, youth group members, church members, school teachers, and youth leaders. When their lists are complete, tell the participants to rate the level of trust in each relationship they listed on a scale of 1 to 10 (10 being high trust level, 1 being very low). Assure them that they will not have to share these lists with anyone. The goal of this exercise is simply to help them understand more clearly who they trust and why. Once they have finished rating their trust relationships, ask them how their responses would have varied if you had specifically asked them to rate the level of trust they place in each person to keep a confidence or the amount of trust they have in the advice and wisdom of the person. Discuss what this says about the different levels of trust.

Continuing The Program

Center the conversation around the following three themes: Trusting Others, Trusting Yourself, and Trusting God.

Trusting Others

- ❏ *What does it mean to trust a person?*

- ❏ *Do you find it easy or difficult to trust people?*

- ❏ *Must a person first earn your trust or do you trust freely until that trust has been violated?*

- ❏ *Are there some people you trust with some things but not with others? Why?*

- ❏ *How do you feel toward a person who does not keep a promise?*

- ❏ *Have you ever been betrayed by a friend? How did it make you feel?*

- ❏ *Have you ever lost trust in someone but continued your relationship with him or her? Were you able to rebuild the trust?*

- ❏ *Are there special characteristics of persons that you are able to trust more than others?*

8

Trusting Yourself

- ❑ Write the characteristics that you think make a trustworthy person. Apply them to yourself.

- ❑ Do you think people trust you? Why or who not?

- ❑ In what ways do you try to demonstrate to others that you are trustworthy?

- ❑ Would you like to be more trustworthy? What might you do to achieve this goal?

- ❑ Do you think it is necessary to first accept and trust yourself before you can trust others?

- ❑ When you make a promise, are you saying you can be trusted?

- ❑ Are there things that you would not want to be trusted to do? Give examples.

- ❑ Have you ever betrayed someone who trusted you? How did it make you feel? How did it affect your relationship?

Trusting God

- ❑ Do you believe you can trust God?

- ❑ Can God trust you?

- ❑ Have you ever let God down?

- ❑ Has God ever let you down?

- ❑ Do you believe that it is possible for God to show Himself to someone who is unresponsive and does not trust?

- ❑ Read I Chronicles 5:20. What does it say about trusting God?

- ❑ Do you trust the church? In what respects?

Concluding The Program

Close with a prayer of thanks for the trust relationships which have developed within this youth group.

GIVING AND ACCEPTING FORGIVENESS

Forgiveness is a word that helps us talk about the process through which broken relationships are healed. Forgiveness is doing away with whatever has come between people. It does not rid life of hurts and pains; it helps us deal with them in a manner that brings renewal in our relationships.

The objective of this program is to help the youth explore the importance of both accepting forgiveness and applying the same measure of forgiveness to others.

In Preparation

In preparation for this session, spend some time reviewing and considering the statements that you will be presenting to the youth in opening the session. You will need to decide how you want to present the statements to the group. You might either print them out on newsprint and go over them as a group, or make copies of them to give to the participants to answer individually and then go over as a group. You might also review the role-play scenarios and determine how you would respond in such situations.

Opening The Program

Open the program by asking the youth to indicate whether they agree or disagree with the following statements. As you go over them, allow time for the participants to discuss their reasons for agreeing or disagreeing. Encourage them to share their personal experiences in which they found it difficult to forgive themselves or others.

- ❏ *It is easier to forgive someone if you understand that he or she did the act that hurt you with your best interest in mind.*

- ❏ *Offering forgiveness to another helps to decrease your own sense of hurt and guilt.*

- ❏ *Being forgiven helps to decrease your sense of guilt and your need to defend your actions.*

- ❏

- ❏ *<u>Accepting</u> forgiveness from someone can be as difficult as <u>offering</u> forgiveness.*

- ❏ *In order to truly forgive someone, you must be able to <u>forget</u> the hurt he or she caused.*

- ❏ *Sometimes it is as difficult to forgive yourself for the mistakes you've made as it is to forgive others for things they have done that hurt you.*

Continuing The Program

Invite the participants to divide into small conversation groups of four persons each and assign one of the following role-play situations to each group. First, have each group discuss the situation they have been assigned and then prepare a role-play of the situation, which they can later present to the whole group. Because different groups may have the same situation to present, their role-play will add to the group insight as to how different persons might react to the same situation.

Role-Play Situation One

For a long time Karen has felt as if Maria is trying to make her an outcast in their group of friends. Karen is convinced Maria speaks badly about her when she is not around. Because of this, Karen began spending less and less time with the group. When Min, a mutual friend, questioned Karen about never being around anymore, Karen confided in her about her feelings toward Maria. Min turned around and told Maria every-

11

thing Karen said. Now Karen feels betrayed. Min asks her forgiveness, saying she only told Maria those things in an attempt to work out the problem.

Role-Play Situation Two

Jeff promised Carlos weeks before that he would help him with a garage sale. A few days before, Jeff's friend invited him to a football game the same day as the garage sale. Not wanting to miss out on the game, Jeff lied and told Carlos he couldn't make it to the garage sale because he had to help his parents around the house. Carlos sees Jeff's parents that day and discovers Jeff lied. Jeff apologizes and asks Carlos' forgiveness.

Role-Play Situation Three

After several months of dating, Jon suddenly breaks up with Andrea. Andrea is very hurt and confused and turns to her best friend Jennifer for support. Jennifer listens but seems very defensive about Jon. A week later Andrea finds out Jennifer and Jon have started dating. They insist that they weren't seeing each other before the break up, but Andrea still feels betrayed. They ask Andrea to forgive them.

Allow time for the groups to work out their role-play situation. This may take 20 or 30 minutes. Then invite each group to present their role-play to the whole group. Follow each role-play presentation with group conversation about how the persons involved handled their situation. In your discussions, ask them whom they would be most likely to forgive and why.

Concluding The Program

In closing the program, share the line from the Lord's Prayer, "And forgive us our debts, as we also have forgiven our debtors." Discuss the biblical verse with the group and encourage them to ponder how they can relate it to their own lives.

COMMUNICATION IS THE KEY

Effective communication is the key to developing and maintaining meaningful relationships. Like meaningful relationships, communication is something that requires a great deal of effort and energy. Truly listening to understand what another person is trying to say is a demanding task, as is expressing yourself effectively. An attitude of respect for others' opinions is also necessary to keep communication flowing.

Communication is also complicated because it is not always achieved simply through words. A person's tone of voice, facial expression or posture can say a lot about the message he or she is trying to convey. The goal of this program is to help the youth recognize the different ways in which they communicate and to understand the importance of listening.

In Preparation

Prepare for this program by considering how effective the communication typically is between the youth group members and between you and the youth. What clues might you glean for improving this communication from the activities and discussion that will take place during the session?

Opening The Program

Open the program by asking the youth to indicate whether they agree or disagree with the following statements about communication. Assure the participants that there is no right or wrong response to these statements. The point of the exercise is to foster discussion, and therefore the youth should be encouraged to share their reasons for responding to the statements the way they did. Invite the participants to share personal experiences which the statements bring to mind.

❏ *A breakdown in communication can be the result of either the speaker not expressing him or herself well, or the listener not really listening.*

❏ *It is easier to communicate with others if you put yourself in their shoes to try and feel how they do.*

❏ *There is a difference between communicating with and communicating to another person.*

❏ *It is difficult to always listen to someone who talks all the time.*

❏ *The subject of conversation has a lot to do with whether you really listen or not. There is a difference between listening to someone and truly hearing what he or she is saying.*

❏ *Sometimes it is difficult to really listen to people you know very well, because you think you already know what they are going to say.*

❏ *No two people ever hear and interpret a message in exactly the same way.*

Continuing The Program

As the group is discussing the statements and sharing personal experiences, you might unexpectedly ask someone to repeat what the last speaker said. It will be interesting to see whether his/her description is accurate according to the last speaker. Try as many of the following exercises as time allows as you continue to explore the art of communicating.

1 Have magazine pictures available of persons interacting and ask each youth to choose one. Tell them to fill in the dialogue by looking at the people depicted and determining whether this is a serious or casual conversation. Ask: Was this a difficult task? What things made it possible to guess what the people were talking about without being able to hear the

conversation? Have the youth share the dialogue they created and see if the other participants agree with them.

2 Divide the youth into two groups. In turn, have each group select a feeling to express, such as fear, sadness, restlessness, happiness, anger or anxiety, without saying a word. Is it easy or difficult for the other group to guess what they are trying to communicate? Do any of the youth seem to be communicating more than one message without realizing it? Ask the youth to identify the nonverbal messages used such as posture, facial expression or gestures.

3 Tell the group a short story twice. The first time have them listen with their eyes covered. The second time have them listen with their ears plugged. Do they get two different stories?

4 Ask the youth to think of an ideal listener they know. Then ask them to think of someone whom they don't think really cares about what they have to say. Ask: What qualities would you use to describe each of these people? Which person are you more like when it comes to listening?

5 Ask the youth to imagine that they want to communicate with another person who they think might not understand what they mean. Given what they have discovered during this program, have the youth discuss how they would go about expressing the thought.

Concluding The Program

Conclude the program by inviting the participants to share what they learned during this session about the importance of communication in building and maintaining relationships. Close with a short prayer praising God for listening to our prayers.

PEOPLE, NOT PUPPETS

It is not an easy world in which to live. There is hunger, home-lessness, racism, pain and suffering. Such injustices can lead people of all ages to question: "If God loves us, then why is there so much suffering in the world?" For adolescents, per-sonal crises can seem so overwhelming that they wonder "Why did God do this to me?" Indeed, our beliefs are often challenged by the question of why pain and suffering exist in a world we know to be created by a loving God.

The goal of this program is to help youth understand that there is no simple understanding of God's ways. What we do know is that He chose to make us free willed people instead of puppets that He could manipulate. This freedom is precious but with it comes an uncertainty about what the future holds.

In Preparation

In preparation for this program, spend some time considering the emotional and spiritual issues involved with this subject. As you have likely discovered, the problem of suffering is not an easy one to handle because there are no simple an-swers. Consider the questions you have had about God's role in suffering which you might share with the group. Also, if there has been a tragedy—either locally or nationally—that has touched the lives of your youth group members, you might use that as a springboard for discussion.

Opening The Program

Open the program by asking the youth to indicate whether they agree or disagree with the following statements. As you go over them, allow time for the participants to discuss their reasons for agreeing or disagreeing. Encourage them to share times their faith has been challenged by questions of "why bad things happen to good people."

❏ *Free will really means being responsible for our actions because what we do affects other people and the rest of God's creation in very profound ways.*

❏ *The problems of suffering profoundly confront our faith and challenge our beliefs.*

❏ *Because we are human, we are limited in our ability to understand God's ways. Much of the injustice we see is caused by people and could be alleviated by people.*

❏ *Explaining the occurrence of human suffering and injustice as the will of God is simply a way of placing all the blame on God.*

❏ *It is possible that God finds excitement in the risk of uncertainty as He gives the future an openness through the freedom of choice which He gives us.*

❏ *When we suffer, God suffers along with us.*

❏ *Our lives are predetermined. We have no say about what direction our lives go.*

Continuing The Program

Continue the conversation by posing the following two questions about freedom:

❏ *What would life be like if God controlled your every decision?*

❏ *Would you rather be a person* having no easy answers or a puppet that has no freedom but doesn't have to make decisions?

Then invite the group to divide into small conversation groups of four per-

17

sons each and assign one of the following role-play situations to each group. First, have each group discuss the situation they have been assigned and then prepare a role-play of the situation, which they can later present to the whole group. Because different groups may have the same situation to present, their role-play will add to the group insight as to how different persons might react to the same situation.

Role-Play Situation One

Stella's baby sister Annie has been ill for several months. When Annie became so sick she had to be hospitalized, it was discovered that the three-year-old has cancer. Doctors believe that with chemotherapy they may be able to prolong Annie's life but only as long as two years. Stella asks you what her family has done to be punished by God like this.

Role-Play Situation Two

After dating for a year, Juan began pressuring Tina to have sex with him. Because Tina was afraid of losing Juan, she gave into him. Two months later she finds out she is pregnant. Now Juan doesn't want to have anything to do with her, and her parents want to send her away to a home for teenage mothers. Tina asks, "Why did God do this to me?"

Role-Play Situation Three

For years Tony's parents have been having problems. They have finally decided they can't work things out and they are getting a divorce. Tony's mother has decided she wants to move to another state to be close to her parents, and Tony has to go with her. Tony doesn't want to leave his girlfriend and all his friends to start all over again at another high school. He keeps talking about how it isn't fair that God let this happen to him.

Allow time for the groups to work out their role-play situation. This may take 20 or 30 minutes. Then invite each group to present their role-play to the whole group. Follow each role-play presentation with group conversation about how the persons involved handled the situation. In your discussions, ask them whose situation would be easier to handle and why.

Concluding The Program

Conclude the program by reassuring the youth that having doubts about God is normal and in no way means they are lacking faith. Encourage the youth to search through the Bible in the coming week for examples of people who experienced doubt. Remember to write them down to share what they discover at future gatherings.

That's What Friends Are For

Everyone wants and needs to have friends. All humans have an overwhelming need to be listened to, accepted and understood. This is particularly true for adolescents as they become more independent and develop additional interests outside the family. Relationships with peers become the main source from which they seek this understanding and acceptance.

The goal of this program is to help youth become better aware of the things they value in a friend and at the same time more conscious of the type of friendship they may be offering others.

In Preparation

In preparation for this program, spend some time thinking about your friendships. How do the friendships in which you are involved differ from each other? Do you rely on some friends for one thing, such as listening or giving sound advice, while counting on other friends for another thing, such as having a good time together? Which friendship do you value most? What quality makes this friendship so valuable?

Also spend some time thinking about the youth involved in your group. Are there some who seem to be especially popular while others have few friends? Recall situations from your past which you can relate concerning popular and un-

20

popular people. Consider how you might provide insights that will prove helpful in building meaningful relationships for the various youth.

Opening The Program

Open the program by asking the youth to indicate whether they agree or disagree with the following statements. As you go over them, allow time for the participants to discuss their reasons for agreeing or disagreeing. Encourage them to share experiences they have had that may have influenced their response to the statements.

❑ *It is more important to have a few close friends than lots of casual friends.*

❑ *As Ralph Waldo Emerson once said, "The only way to have a friend is to be one."*

❑ *Few people know how to really be a friend.*

❑ *You can't have a friendship without trust.*

❑ *Honesty is the single most important thing in a friendship.*

❑ *Everybody needs friends, no matter how independent they may be.*

Continuing The Program

Continue the conversation by posing some of the following questions:

❑ *What qualities do you look for in a good friend?*

❑ *What makes you a good friend?*

❑ *Name a rule you have found important in making and maintaining friendships.*

❑ *Proverbs 17:17 says: "A friend loves at all times, and kinsfolk are born to share adversity." What clues does this give you about what it means to be a real friend?*

❑ *How important to you is having friends? What matters more to you—having lots of friends or having a few close friends who you can always count on?*

21

❑ *Is having friends important enough to you that you are willing to take the risk of pursuing new relationships?*

❑ *How do you go about making new friends?*

❑ *Does having friends make you feel as if there is no crises you can't overcome or do you believe that you can never really depend on anybody but yourself to get through the rough times?*

❑ *What is the main thing you need to work on when it comes to forming friendships and maintaining them?*

❑ *Do you believe that in some cases our friends make us who we are? Have you ever found yourself behaving like your*

❑ *friends? Do you think this change in yourself was positive or negative—did it make you a better or worse person?*

❑ *Does being a true friend mean having to accept the imperfections of others?*

❑ *Do you rely on different friends for different things? Is there one friend you might turn to for advice and another friend you go to when you need to be cheered up? What type of a friend do you think others perceive you as?*

❑ *What is the best thing a friend ever did for you? What is the worst thing a friend ever did to you? What did these experiences show you about being a friend?*

Concluding The Program

Conclude the program by having one of the youth read Matthew 7:12 aloud, followed by a few moments of silence.

22

AIDS::
ATTITUDES AND ACTIONS

It is inevitable that most youth's lives will be touched by AIDS in one way or another. Surveys tell us that the main routes of AIDS infection—unsafe sexual contact and needle sharing in drug use—involve activities practiced by a high percentage of youth. And the number of people of all ages who are infected with the AIDS virus continues to grow. For these reasons, it is essential that the church not only be a source of education on the disease but also a model of how Christians can reach out to people with AIDS and show them God's compassionate and unconditional love.

This program will give youth an opportunity to explore their own attitudes about AIDS as well as actions they might take in supporting those infected or affected by the disease.

In Preparation

The experiences of the participants in your youth group will greatly affect how this program takes shape. As facilitator of the group, you should spend some time thinking about the youth group members and considering if any of them have had a friend or family member stricken with AIDS. If so, be sure to be sensitive to their feelings during this youth program and allow them to share their experiences only if they wish to do so. Depending on how well the participants know one another and how open they are with each other, the discussions might also focus on youth who have feared they contracted the AIDS virus. Again, this discussion should be initiated by the youth themselves and the group should be reminded that nothing that is said during the program should be repeated.

You may want to allow some time during the program for sharing basic information about AIDS as well as current statistics. A monthly record of the statistics on AIDS is available free by writing to the Centers For Disease Control, c/o Public Health Service, Atlanta, GA 30333.

Opening The Program

Open the program by focusing on Magic Johnson or another celebrity being infected with the HIV virus that causes AIDS. (If there is someone in your church or community that the youth know has AIDS, you might choose instead to focus on him or her.) Ask the youth to share how the news of Magic's diagnosis affected them. Did it surprise them to see that anyone can be HIV positive, not just homosexuals or drug users? How did this realization affect the way they now look at people with AIDS? Did it make them at all fearful of contracting the disease? Try to draw conversation from each member of the group.

Continuing The Program

Any or all of the following questions may be posed to help continue the discussion.

❑ *Once symptoms of AIDS become evident, the resulting physical problems can cause rapid loss of job, insurance coverage, family relationships and friendships. Which of these losses do you think would be most devastating?*

❑ *How do you think a person's ability to cope with AIDS might be affected by their loved ones'* *attitudes about the disease?*

❑ *Would you agree that having AIDS is even more traumatic than having most other terminal illnesses because it is a disease which is feared and misunderstood by the majority of the population? How might a person with cancer, for instance, be treated differently than someone with AIDS? How do*

24

you think this would affect the quality of their remaining days?

❑ Which of the following things would you feel comfortable doing with a person with AIDS?
___talking ___eating
___hugging ___kissing

❑ Which of the following, if any, do you think should be required to be tested for AIDS?
___physicians
___dentists
___teachers
___restaurant cooks & servers
___hairdressers

❑ Would you refuse to use or hire any of the above people if you knew they had AIDS?

❑ Do you think that gaining a clear understanding of the psychological and infection issues can help people deal better with people who have AIDS?

❑ Have your feelings about AIDS or your attitude toward people with AIDS been changed by anything you've learned in the last few years?

❑ How do you respond to people who say that AIDS is God's way of punishing people for their promiscuous behavior?

❑ What is your school doing in terms of AIDS education? Do you think this is adequate? What more would you like to see done?

❑ What role, if any, do you think the church should play in educating people about AIDS?

❑ What is your church currently doing with regards to helping people understand AIDS or supporting people with AIDS and their families? What other programs would you suggest and/or be willing to help develop?

Concluding The Program

Conclude the session by spending a few minutes having the youth express their concerns to God in prayer. Encourage them to take action on some of the things they thought of to help people with AIDS.

Honesty

Being absolutely honest all of the time can be difficult, if not down right impossible. As humans we have a natural tendency to want to protect ourselves or others, and that can sometimes lead us to be less than honest.

It is important to discuss honesty with youth because they have reached a point in their lives where dishonesty becomes much more significant than just telling lies to get what they want. Now they begin to see honesty as a value and they must decide how important this value is for their lives.

In Preparation

In preparation for this program, spend some time reviewing and considering the statements that you will be presenting to the youth in opening this program. Also reflect on how honest you are with others. Think back to your adolescent years and take note of any examples you can share with the group of times you were dishonest and what happened as a result. Relaying personal stories will help the group identify with you and will give you insight into their mindset.

Opening The Program

Open the program by asking the youth to indicate whether they agree or disagree with the following statements about honesty. Assure the participants that there is no right or wrong response to these statements. The point of the exercise is to foster discussion, and therefore the youth should be encouraged to share their reasons for responding to the statements the way they did. Invite the participants to share personal experiences which the statements bring to mind.

❑ *Honesty is always the best policy.*

❑ *People are more respected when they are completely honest all of the time.*

❑ *There are some things better left unsaid, even if it means being dishonest.*

❑ *Being in a trust relationship with*

someone means trusting them to always tell us the truth.

❑ *It takes time for trust to be developed in a relationship, but it only takes one moment of dishonesty to destroy it.*

❑ *To be Christian means to be honest and trustworthy.*

Continuing The Program

Continue the conversation by posing the following questions:

❑ *Is honesty always the best policy, or are there times when it is better to tell a "small lie" rather than be honest and risk hurting someone's feelings?*

❑ *Would you rather have someone be dishonest with you in order to spare your feelings, or would you prefer the truth no matter how it makes you feel?*

❑ *Would you be able to trust a friend who you discovered had been dishonest with you? Would it matter if he or she had lied to spare your feelings?*

❑ *Do you think people can be honest with each other all of the time and still get along?*

❑ *Do you think it is hard or easy to be yourself all of the time? How does this affect your honesty with others?*

❑ *How do you feel after you have told a lie?*

❑ *What keeps you from lying? Would you lie more if you knew that you would not get caught?*

❑ *Has there ever been a time when you learned the true meaning of* the saying, "Oh what a tangled web we weave when first we practice to deceive"? Have you ever told what you thought to be a "small lie", but it kept growing as you tried covering it up?

❑ Is there such thing as a "little white lie"?

❑ Is it dishonest to not tell someone something you know

that affects him or her?

❑ Who of the following do you find it most difficult to be honest with and why?

_____siblings
_____parents
_____peers
_____friends
_____teachers

Now tell the group you are going to give them some examples of dishonesty. They should go to the right side of the room if they think the lie is harmless or go to the left side if they think it is serious. When the group has separated to different sides of the room, allow them time to discuss their viewpoints before you read off another example.

❑ Cheating on a test.

❑ Lying to protect someone's feelings.

❑ Giving insincere compliments.

❑ Embellishing a story to impress

others.

❑ Lying to your parents to protect yourself from punishment.

❑ Giving a teacher an untrue excuse for turning in a paper late.

When this exercise is concluded, point out that one of the dangers of dishonesty is that one lie tends to lead to another. Illustrate this by having the group expand on the scenarios listed above. Using the first scenario as an example, point out that the person's first act of dishonesty is cheating. Suppose the teacher finds the cheat sheet but the student lies about it, saying it was her study sheet and she didn't realize it was on her desk. If the teacher does not believe her, she will either have to admit the truth or face lying to her parents as well. Where will the lying end?

Concluding The Program

Invite one of the participants to read Acts 5:1-4 aloud. Suggest that the youth reflect on what this passage says about Christianity and honesty during the coming week.

FACING FAILURE

Failure is an inevitable part of life for those who are willing to take risks. Yet it is only through risk taking that we are able to grow and attain our goals. The times when we fail, however, can be difficult and painful.

It is important that adolescents be helped to understand that both failures and successes are important parts of growing and attaining goals. Failure may become more bearable if the youth come to accept their limitations. Every race, game or competition will show that some people excel more than others. By accepting both their strengths and weaknesses, youth may be more realistic about the success they may hope to achieve. At the same time, by looking at past failures, they may come to see how they have learned from these experiences and benefited from the risk of trying.

In Preparation

In preparation for this program, spend some time reviewing and considering the statements that you will be presenting to the youth in opening the program. Also spend some time thinking about painful defeats you have experienced. You might particularly try to recall a time that you failed but were able to gain something from the experience. The youth may be interested in hearing some of these insights during the program.

Opening The Program

Open the program by asking the youth to indicate whether they agree or disagree with the following statements about success and failure. Assure the participants that there are no right or wrong responses to these statements. The point of the exercise is to foster discussion, and therefore the youth should be encouraged to share their reasons for responding to the statements the way they did. Invite the participants to share personal experiences which the statements bring to mind.

❑ *The most important thing in life is succeeding.*

❑ *A person can learn something about him/herself through defeat.*

❑ *Caring and trying are not always enough to succeed at everything.*

❑ *One of the biggest failures*

people face is the failure to go after their dreams.

❑ *Failure is the opposite of success.*

❑ *Avoiding the embarrassment of failure is more important than the chance for success.*

Continuing The Program

Invite those youth who wish to share the most painful defeat they have ever experienced. Encourage them to relate what, if anything, they learned from it. Continue the conversation by posing the following questions:

❑ *Are there particular things you are more likely to fail at than others? Does this knowledge keep you from trying or simply help to lessen the disappointment?*

❑ *Are you concerned about how others view your failures?*

❑ *Are you more concerned about your successes and failures or about how they are viewed by others?*

❑ *Do you judge your success at things according to your own set of goals or in comparison to other people's successes?*

❑ *Is it worth taking chances, despite the possibility of failure?*

❑ *Are you satisfied with the risks you are taking in life? What other risks would you be taking if you were guaranteed that you would succeed?*

❑ *Do you think your faith makes a difference in how you face failure? Are there certain ways in which your faith helps you to cope?*

❑ *Do you think God cares whether*

you succeed or fail? Do you think God sees people as successes and failures?

❑ *Have you ever had an experience in which an apparent failure turned into a success or a success turned into a failure?*

❑ *What do you think are the most common causes of failure? Discuss bad luck, lack of skill or talent, insufficient preparation, carelessness, injustice.*

After discussing the above questions, pass out paper and pencils and ask the youth to each make a list of the things they would most like to accomplish in their lives, such as popularity, good grades, strong family relationships or sports achievements. When their lists are complete, have them consider ways in which they may strive to attain those goals. Then invite them to think of a time when their attempts in one of the areas listed did not work out. Ask them to consider how the experience affected their ability to attain the goal in the future. Did it keep them from ever being able to be successful? Or did the experience help them to see better how they may be able to attain the goal? Was it worth trying?

Concluding The Program

In closing, remind the youth that failure is an unavoidable risk in attempting to achieve goals. Whether they fail or succeed in their attempts, they can always be winners if they strive to gain something from the experience.

Alone Or Lonely?

It is odd to think that, in a world with so many people, loneliness exists. Yet it is a fact that as our society becomes increasingly urbanized, genuine community actually becomes more difficult to find and maintain. Thus, people of all ages may experience loneliness at one time or another. During adolescence these feelings of loneliness may be magnified by lack of self-esteem and pressure to fit in.

The goal of this program is to give the youth a chance talk about their lonely feelings, the causes and cures of loneliness and the value of being alone.

In Preparation

In your preparation for this program spend some time reflecting on past experiences of loneliness. Consider if there was any particular occurrence in your life that brought on these feelings. Try recalling a time when your loneliness was situational—such as following the loss of a loved one—as well as when it stemmed from your own feelings of aloneness. You may share these insights with the youth during the program as a means of illustrating that everyone experiences loneliness at one time or another.

You should also spend some time before the program thinking about each of the participants. Do any of the youth strike you as being lonely or even loners? If so, be sure to be sensitive to their feelings during the program.

Opening The Program

Begin the program by inviting the youth to each write an acrostic poem using the word ALONE. Pass out paper and pencils for them to write their poems, assuring them that they will not have to share theirs with the group unless they wish to. When the participants are done writing, allow those who choose to read their poems aloud. Then read the two below as a means of bringing out different people's ideas about being alone.

Aimlessly

Looking for

One to

Notice me

Everywhere, anywhere

A chance to

Look at my life

Or just relax with

No interruptions

Except my own thoughts

As follow-up to discussing the poems, ask the youth to indicate whether they agree or disagree with the following statements. Assure the participants that there are no right or wrong responses to these statements. The point of the exercise is to foster discussion, and therefore the youth should be encouraged to share their reasons for responding to the statements the way they did.

❑ *Everyone is lonely at times during their lives.*

❑ *Being alone and being lonely are two different things.*

34

- ❏ *It is possible for someone to be a loner and never feel estranged.*

- ❏ *If you are always with people, you won't get lonely.*

- ❏ *It is not always possible to know what causes lonely feelings.*

- ❏ *Being alone every once in a while is important.*

Participating in these two activities should help the youth see that there is a difference between being alone and being lonely. Explain to the group that the purpose of this program is to explore feelings of loneliness as well as the value of being alone.

Continuing The Program

Invite those youth who wish to share personal experiences of loneliness. Continue the conversation by posing the following questions:

- ❏ *Have you ever been in a large crowd yet felt completely alone? Can you explain how you felt?*

- ❏ *Do you believe a person can prevent loneliness? If so, share specific ways.*

- ❏ *What type of person does not appear to ever be lonely? Can you always depend on appearances when it comes to detecting loneliness?*

- ❏ *When someone appears to be lonely, what, if anything, do you do to help them?*

- ❏ *Has someone ever done anything to help you when you were feeling lonely? What?*

- ❏ *Who do you think are the loneliest people in the world?*

- ❏ *Are there times when you enjoy being alone?*

- ❏ *What other feelings do you associate with the experience of loneliness? (e.g., rejection, sadness, hurt, bitterness, depression) How do these feelings differ from those that you feel when alone?*

- ❏ *What are the positive values of being alone? Why do you think Jesus sought to be alone in Mark 1:35?*

Now brainstorm as a group practical solutions to loneliness. (Example: praying, enjoying solitude, talking with parents, reaching out to help others, making and maintaining friendships, developing hobbies, accomplishing tasks that have been put off.)

Concluding The Program

In closing, encourage the youth to start taking time out each week to be alone with themselves away from the distractions of people, television or radio. Suggest that they use this time to pray or just to think.

VALUES TO LIVE BY

Few things impact the way we live our lives as much as our values. Values are important in setting our priorities and helping us make decisions. Yet the values that we say we believe in might be different from the values that we live by. We might say we value honesty yet we may cheat on an exam or fail to point out to a salesclerk that he has undercharged us. Adolescence is the time in one's life when there is usually the greatest inconsistency between what one believes and what one does. This program is designed to help youth explore and share the struggles they face as they try to live by the values they deem important.

A person's values are developed over a period of many years and have been influenced by family members, friends, school, church and the media. This program will also give the youth an opportunity to discover how they form the values they hold.

In Preparation

In preparation for this program, spend some time thinking about the things you deem most important in life. You might try making a list of your highest personal values and then review them to see if you can determine what experiences in life may have led you to place such importance on them. Also consider how your values have changed over the years and why.

37

Spend some time also thinking about times when your behavior has not directly reflected your values. You might want to share an example with the youth as a means of illustrating that no one is perfect and that it is normal to believe in something but not be able to live it all of the time.

Opening The Program

Begin the program by inviting the participants to each list their highest personal values, such as personal achievement, religion, education, honesty, equality. When they have completed their lists, ask them to go back and rate the values in order of importance. Invite them to think about why they hold these things in high value and what person or group influenced their thinking. Then, for each of the items on the list, tell them to consider if they are able to live by that value all of the time, the majority of the time, some of the time, or none of the time. Because this may leave some of the youth feeling guilty, you might take this opportunity to share your personal struggles with living by your values.

Continuing The Program

Continue the conversation by posing the following questions about living by our values:

❑ *Do you believe that what one values determines how one lives in the world? Have you ever done something that conflicted with your values? Share the experience.*

❑ *How did you feel behaving in a way that conflicted with the values you hold? Why do you think you sometimes do things even though you believe it is wrong?*

Now that the youth have begun to explore the values they hold and how they affect their living, spend some time focusing on the way in which values are formed. Ask:

❑ *Who have been the key people in helping you form values? How*

have your values changed over the years?

- *There is an old phrase that says, "Values are caught, not taught." What do you think this says about the way in which we are influenced by others?*

- *Rank the following according to how much influence you feel they have on your values:*
  ___Family members ___Friends ___School ___Church ___Media

- *Would you have ranked this list differently five years ago? How about just one year ago? Why?*

- *Compare your values to those of your parents. Have you adopted many of their values? Consider conflicts that have occurred between you and your parents recently. Did any of these problems have anything to do with differences between your parents' values and your own?*

- *Imagine that you are a parent. What are the most important values you want to pass along to your children? What will you do to demonstrate to your children how important these values are?*

- *Do you believe you have had an impact on any specific person's values? If so, how does this make you feel?*

- *Who is your role model? Are his or her values important to you?*

Concluding The Program

In concluding the program, encourage the youth to consider ways they may better reflect the personal values they hold. Assure them that it is perfectly normal to struggle between what we believe and how we live, but our goal should always be to come closer to living by our values. To help them to this end, select one value as a group and brainstorm ways in which they can put this value to work in their lives. Encourage them to try this in the coming week and share results at the next meeting.

PRAYER

Communication is the key to any relationship, including the one we share with God. Prayer is the way we talk with and listen to God. Without prayer, it is difficult for God to have a presence in our lives. Yet the importance of prayer is often not recognized by youth. They may question whether God actually hears their prayers or responds. Others may think they don't need to pray or don't pray even if they think they should. Through the discussion and activities in this program, the youth will gain insight into the importance of prayer and how it can bring them closer to God.

In Preparation

In preparing for this session, spend some time reflecting on your own prayer life. How important is prayer to you today? How does this differ from when you were an adolescent? Recall any times when you doubted that God listened to your prayers. Take note of any examples you might share with the youth during this session. It will be reassuring for them to hear that someone with a satisfying prayer life has had doubts along the way. Be sensitive to the fact also that some of the participants may feel guilty when discussing prayer because they don't do it regularly.

Opening The Program

Begin the program by inviting the members of the group to define the word "prayer" in their own words. Jot down the different definitions on newsprint or a chalkboard. Spend a few minutes discussing these definitions as they are suggested. Ask: Do you believe prayer must have a certain structure or follow a certain pattern or *can* it be more of a conversation with God? Point out during this discussion that people can pray silently at any time without closing their eyes, bowing their heads or using formal language.

Continuing The Program

Continue the conversation by asking the following questions:

❑ *Do you think you pray more or less than most people your age?*

❑ *Are you satisfied with your prayer life?*

❑ *Why do you or don't you pray? What blocks have you discovered that are in your way of prayer?*

❑ *Do you feel guilty for not praying?*

❑ *Which of the following is most often your motivation for praying?*
___*asking for something*
___*thanking God*
___*seeking guidance on important decisions*

___*maintaining a relationship with God*
___*praising God*
___*seeking forgiveness*

❑ *If you could pray for only one thing, what would it be?*

❑ *What type of prayer rituals did you have as a child, such as praying before meals or before bedtime? Do you still continue these rituals today? Why or why not?*

❑ *Do you pray most when you are alone or with groups, such as in church?*

❑ *Do you feel comfortable praying in public?*

- Do you pray for others as well as for yourself?

- Do you ever ask others to pray for you? Do you believe that it helps to have others pray for you?

Continue the session by shifting the focus to God's response to our prayers. The following questions may help in fostering discussion:

- Recall an experience of answered prayer. Was it answered the way you wanted or expected? Did the answer come right away? In what way did it come?

- There is a country western song with lyrics that say "Sometimes I thank God for unanswered prayers." Have you ever been thankful that you did not get something you prayed for? Do you think not getting it was a reflection of God's infinite wisdom or merely a coincidence?

- Do you believe that God hears all prayers even if they go unanswered?

Ask: Do you believe prayer can serve as a healing tool? Larry Dossey, M.D., a former chief of staff at Medical City Dallas Hospital in Texas and author of Healing Words: The Power of Prayer and the Practice of Medicine (Harper San Francisco, 1993) has found more than 130 studies tying prayer with recoveries from heart disease, wounds and other ailments. Some scientists suggest that the process of praying merely calms people enough to allow their bodies to heal. However, that does not explain why people who do not pray for themselves but have others praying for them also heal more quickly. A San Francisco hospital study demonstrated how heart patients who were prayed for suffered fewer complications. What do you believe is the explanation for this? Do you have any personal experience with the healing power of prayer?

Now as a group compile a prayer request list. Invite the youth to name things or people they would like one another to pray for in the coming week. Requests can be as general as "world peace" or as specific as "my aunt who is recovering from surgery." When everyone has offered a request, encourage the youth to remember these people and things in their prayers.

Concluding The Program

Conclude the program by offering a few minutes of silence for the youth to pray.

Love Yourself And Love Others

"Love your neighbor as yourself" implies a package deal. It sug-
gests that in order to love others, you must first love yourself.
Yet the adolescent years are times of uncertainty, confusion and
personal evaluation. Youth, as with many people of all ages,
often lack self-confidence and are not at peace with who they
are. This struggle to accept and love themselves can make ac-
cepting and loving others very difficult.

This program is aimed at looking not only at our self-concept
but how that self-concept affects the relationships that we have.
It will help youth gain an understanding of how feeling better
about themselves can make relationships easier for them.

In Preparation

As leader, you might prepare for this program by thinking about times in
your life when you doubted your own worth or lacked self-confidence. Consider
how your self-concept affected the way you behaved toward the people with
whom you came in contact. Was there a time you can think of when you really felt
at peace with yourself? How did this positive attitude affect your relationships?
These reflections might interest the participants and encourage discussion during
the program.

Opening The Program

On newsprint or a chalkboard, have the following quote by Bertrand Flussell printed large enough for the participants to read: "A man cannot possibly be at peace with others until he has learned to be at peace with himself." As the youth arrive, give them some time to consider the statement. Then spend a few minutes discussing their reaction to it. See how many in your group agree with the statement and then ask several persons to briefly explain why they agree. There may be participants who disagree with the statement. Be sure to offer them an opportunity to share their reasons also. Encourage all the participants to consider how the way they feel about themselves affects the way they treat others.

Foster discussion by asking the following questions:

❑ *What does the phrase "Love your neighbor as yourself " say to you? Does it imply that it is necessary to love yourself in order to love others?*

❑ *Are there people you can think of who don't seem to accept you? What type of image do these people appear to have of themselves?*

❑ *Are there people you have trouble accepting? What are your reasons for not loving or accepting these people? Do you think your relationship with these people could be improved if you took the initiative and tried to accept them for who they are? Would this be easier if you felt better about yourself?*

❑ *Can you recall a time when the way you felt about yourself affected the way you treated those around you? Do the relationships you are in seem better when you are feeling good about yourself?*

❑ *Must the love be returned in order for you to love someone?*

Continuing The Program

Continue the program by introducing the following exercise which should help clarify for the youth the parts of themselves they value and the parts with which they are unhappy.

Give the participants paper and pencils and have them make lists of the ten words or phrases that describe the most important features of who they are. The list can include social roles, physical characteristics, intellectual characteristics, specific skills, attitudes or belief systems.

When all the lists are completed, ask the participants to choose the one item from their lists that is most fundamental to who they are and copy it on the back of their paper. They should continue ranking the ten items until they have reorganized them all. Now have the participants close their eyes and create a mental image of themselves. Ask them to recall the item they ranked as least important and imagine this item suddenly disappearing from their personality or physical make-up. Ask them to consider how losing this tenth item would affect the way they act, the way they feel, the way others behave toward them, and the way they might behave toward others. Was it easy to give up that item? Do they like themselves more or less without it?

Continue by having them remove item nine. Ask: What difference does its absence make for you and your relationships? Continue the process by removing one item at a time until they have given them all up.

After participants have expressed their initial reactions to this exercise, follow up by discussing these questions:

❑ *Which was the most difficult element of yourself to give up? What makes you value this aspect of yourself so highly? Do you think this aspect is something that makes others respect and accept you?*

❑ *Which was the easiest element of yourself to give up? Did you like yourself better without it? Why or why not?*

❑ *Was there a point in "removing" elements from your make-up that you felt better about yourself than you normally do? Or did you find it difficult to give up elements because you are happy with yourself?*

Concluding The Program

Ask the group members to write letters to themselves in which they remind themselves of their positive qualities and characteristics. Collect these letters and mail back to the authors at a later date.

LIVE EACH MOMENT

*What would you do differently if you had your life to live over?
While most people's responses to that question vary widely,
there are usually some common threads tying them together:
they would take more chances, grasp more opportunities..."live
life more fully." Too often, however, the risk of trying something
different prevents us from living the way we'd really like to. This
is particularly true for youth, who often struggle with low self-esteem and peer pressure.*

*This program is designed to help your youth group members con-
sider the influences in their lives that keep them from taking
risks and "living life more fully."*

In Preparation

In preparation for this program, spend some time reflecting on experiences when fears or insecurities have kept you from trying something new. Focus specifically on your adolescent years and try to recall a time when you failed to take a risk. If you could go back and do it over, would you take the chance? Share your insights with the group during the course of this youth program.

Opening The Program

Begin the program by reading the following poem which Bernie Siegel, the well-known cancer surgeon, shared in his book <u>Peace, Love & Healing</u>.[1] Explain to the youth that it was written by an 85-year-old woman who was facing death.

If I had my life to live over, I'd try
To make more mistakes next time. I would
Relax, I would limber up, I would be crazier
Than I've been on this trip. I know very
Few things I'd take seriously any more.
I would take more chances, I would take more
Trips, I would scale more mountains,
I would swim more rivers, and I would
Watch more sunsets. I would eat more
Ice cream and fewer beans.
I would have more actual troubles
And fewer imaginary ones. You see...
I was one of those people who lived
Prophylactically and sensibly and sanely,
Hour after hour and day after day.
Oh, I've had my moments
And if I had it to do all over
Again, I'd have many more of them.
In fact, I'd try not to have anything
Else, just moments, one after another,
Instead of living so many
Years ahead of my day. I've been
One of those people who never went anywhere without
A thermometer, a hot water bottle, a gargle, a
Raincoat and a parachute.
If I had it to do all over again,
I'd travel lighter, much lighter,
Than I have.
I would start barefoot earlier

In the spring, and I'd stay that way
Later in the fall. And I would
Ride more merry-go-rounds, and
Catch more gold rings, and greet
More people, and pick more flowers,
And dance more often. If I had it
To do all over again.
But you see,
I don't.

Invite the youth to share their feelings about the poem. Foster discussion by posing the following questions:

❑ *What do you think the woman was implying by writing, "I'd try to make more mistakes next time"? Do you think it is possible to prepare too much and approach new experiences too cautiously? Do you consider all the possible outcomes before making a change or doing something different or unusual?*

❑ *Can you see the poet's point in saying, "I would have more actual troubles and fewer imaginary ones"? Have you ever felt as if you were spending too much time worrying about things that were not really worth it? Are there things you can think of that you take more seriously than you need to?*

❑ *The woman wrote that she wished she could have nothing but "moments, one after another, instead of living so many years ahead of my day." Do you always consider how your actions will affect your future plans? Is there something that, if you were just living moment by moment, you would do now?*

Continuing The Program

Continue the conversation by pointing out that our fears often keep us from living life to the fullest. There is the fear of the unknown, the fear of standing out in the crowd, and especially the fear of rejection. Youth are often more concerned with "fitting in" than living the way they want to.

50

Have the participants consider risks they have taken in the past by asking them the following questions:

❑ *Think of a time that you were truly impulsive. Did you later regret your impulsiveness?*

❑ *Think of a time when you did something despite the chance of failure. How did it turn out? Were you glad you took the risk?*

❑ *Think of a time when you took the initiative in establishing a new relationship with another person. Were you concerned about being rejected or misunderstood by the other person? Were you glad you took the risk? Have you ever wanted to establish a new relationship but thought that the other person would not want to know you better so you gave up before ever trying?*

Now that the youth are thinking about different risks, give them paper and pencils. Invite them to write short open-ended stories concerned with a particular risk they are hesitant to take. Tell them to end the story with "What would you do?" Have them exchange stories. Allow time for each to read a story aloud and the others to give suggested endings.

Concluding The Program

Conclude the program by inviting the group to respond to the following questions: "What do you wish you could do more of in your life? What is keeping you from doing it?"

[1]Siegel, Bernie. Peace, Love and Healing. Harper & Row Publishers, 1989.

JUST DO IT!

"Just do it" the Nike advertisements so simply assert. Yet most of us at one time or another find it difficult to just jump in and accomplish a task. Instead we fall into the procrastination chain, putting off what should be done today and as a result often neglecting other responsibilities as we struggle to make up for lost time.

The procrastination habit, of course, strikes young and old, but is particularly common among today's active adolescents. They often feel pulled in many directions as they try to meet the demands of school, family, friends, church, etc. Most youth have experienced the consequences of putting things off, but they may still find themselves falling back into the procrastination habit. This program is aimed at helping youth understand the different reasons they may procrastinate.

In Preparation

As facilitator of the group, you should spend some time thinking about times when you have procrastinated. Consider why you put the tasks off and what the resulting consequences were. Then recall the very last time you put off doing something. How long ago was it? Is procrastination something you still often struggle with or have you found some time management techniques that help?

These experiences and techniques will be important to share with the youth during this program.

Opening The Program

There are several approaches you might take in opening this program and introducing the topic of procrastination to the youth. If you have had a particularly poignant experience of the consequences of procrastination, you might begin by sharing this with the group. Or you might tell the group that you waited until the last minute to develop a program for this meeting and unfortunately you were unable to come up with anything. Don't make any excuses for your lack of preparedness but rather admit that you have procrastinated. Experience the embarrassment that such a scenario would bring you if this were truly happening.

A third approach would be to give a Bible study assignment to the youth at a previous meeting. Tell them this doesn't have to be completed for three weeks but that they shouldn't put it off because it will require a lot of time and effort. Then begin this program by asking the youth to share any questions or problems they have found with this project. There is likely to be a number of youth who have yet to begin the project. This should help you lead into a discussion on procrastination. If you use this approach, be sure to give an assignment that can be used as part of a future youth program. You don't want the youth spending their time on a project that is never used.

Whichever approach you use to introduce the topic, be sure then to invite the group members to share experiences they have had with procrastination. Try to draw conversation from each member of the group.

Continuing The Program

Center the program around the following four themes:

1. Delaying Gratification. Share the following story with the youth: In <u>The Road Less Traveled</u>[1] Scott Peck tells the story of a 30-year-old financial analyst who complained over a period of months about her procrastination in her job, yet after all the painstaking psychoanalytic work had been done, she still procrastinated just as much as before. One day Peck asked her, "Do you like cake?" She admitted that she did.

"What part of the cake do you like best?" he continued.

"The frosting," she said with a smile.

"How do you eat a piece of cake?"

"The frosting first, of course!"

From there, her work habits were observed and it was suggested that she force herself to accomplish the unpleasant part of her job first, then she would be free to enjoy the pleasant. Instead of devoting herself to the pleasurable part of the first hour and spending the remaining six hours avoiding the unpleasant part, it was suggested that she force herself to do the one hour of pain first and look forward to the following six hours.

Ask the youth if they can identify with the woman who ate her frosting first. Invite them to share their struggles with completing homework or chores before indulging in pleasurable activities. Do they have trouble delaying gratification in order to complete tasks?

Discuss the motto "Play now, pay later." Do they think this motto applies to procrastination? Invite them to share times when they have had to "pay" for playing.

2. Decisions, Decisions. Discuss with the group how procrastination stems from fear of making a decision. Invite them to share a time when they put off a task because it required making a decision, such as what topic to do a report on or what colleges to apply to. Ask: Did putting off the decision actually help you to make a wiser choice or did it end up being a rushed decision?

Ask the youth if they think that not deciding is actually making a decision. Encourage the participants to share experiences when their hesitancy to make a decision resulted in having the decision made for them because options were no longer available.

3. The Fear Of Failure. Explain that procrastination is rooted in a fear of failure, a fear of not doing the best job possible. Most habitual procrastinators tend to set high standards for themselves which often results in putting off the more difficult chores for fear the results won't live up to expectations. Ask the youth if they have ever found themselves putting off a task because they thought they would be able to do a better job later. Did delaying the task help or hurt the outcome?

Have the participants consider the feelings they experience when they set out to accomplish a task. What keeps them from actually beginning to work on a report when they had first intended? Is fear of failure one of the deterrents?

4. Discipline. Discuss the importance of discipline in overcoming the habit of procrastination. Ask: Do you see value in discipline? Do you ever rebel against it? Do you think people can be too disciplined or too undisciplined? Invite the youth to think of one area in their life in which they would like to be more disciplined. Encourage them to determine one thing they might do to develop this discipline.

Read Hebrews 12:11 as a group. Discuss what this passage says about discipline.

Reassure the youth that it is normal to want to put off the difficult projects in favor of the quick and easy, more enjoyable ones. Encourage the participants to share ways they have found to balance the many things in their lives, such as family, school, work, hobbies, church, friends, etc.

Concluding The Program

Conclude the program by asking the participants to make a vow to do something this week that they have been putting off for a long time. Tell them that it doesn't necessarily have to be school work or a chore, it could be calling a friend, writing a letter, or following up on a job possibility.

[1]Peck, Scott. The Road Less Traveled. (New York: Simon & Schuster, 1978).

Dealing With Depression

Two emotions that characterize depression—discouragement and feelings of inadequacy—might also be used to describe the way adolescents feel as they struggle to fit in. Thus, many of the youth in your group likely have experienced some degree of depression without knowing why. It is important that they understand that the negative things they tell themselves can bring on depression just as much as a traumatic experience or loss might.

This program will help youth explore different causes for depression as well as offer them some ideas for overcoming low spirits. As they consider the things that make them feel down, hopefully they will also glean ways of minimizing future depression.

In Preparation

As facilitator for this program, you should spend some time thinking about the individuals in your group and times when they have seemed down or depressed. Consider whether these feelings seemed to be brought on by a specific event or loss or if they stemmed from a lack of self-worth. Keeping these experiences in mind should help you determine what areas of discussion to spend more time with during the program. If you would like to expand the scope of this program to look at clinical depression, free brochures on symptoms and treatments can be ordered from the National Institute of Mental Health at 1-800-421-4211.

Opening The Program

Open the program by inviting the members to picture in their minds a time they felt down or depressed. Assure them they will not have to share their specific experiences with the group so they should be as honest with themselves as possible. Encourage them to relax and close their eyes as you lead them through this exercise by saying: How do you feel? How are your feelings making you behave? How do you feel toward others? Do you know why you are feeling down? If not, try "stepping out" of yourself to look at yourself as an outsider might. Can you see any reason why the person you are looking at should be depressed?

Now that the youth have a specific experience on which to focus, invite them to share what they think the meaning and causes of depression are. Continue conversation by posing these questions:

❑ *Do you always know what is making you feel down or depressed?*

❑ *Do you feel that depression is something you initiate or is it brought on by outside forces or events in life over which you have little control?*

❑ *Can you talk yourself into depression with the negative thoughts you have?*

❑ *Have you ever felt hurt or depressed from holding in angry feelings?*

❑ *How does depression affect your behavior?*

❑ *Do you think depression can be a sign that you should change something you are doing in your life?*

❑ *Have you ever made a change to help erase feelings of depression?*

❑ *Do you think that unhappiness may stem from an inability to distinguish between what is and what should be? Do you think people who are constantly dreaming about the ideal have a difficult time being satisfied with what they have?*

57

Continuing The Program

Now that the youth have looked at some of the causes of depression, invite those who wish to share some of the things they have done to help bring themselves out of a depressed state. Share some of the following techniques:

Distinguish between self statements that are constructive and those that are overly negative and depressing. *Are there things you say to yourself that make you feel bad or sad? Are the things you say true?*

Do something for which you can feel proud. *Taking on a project and completing it can give you a sense of accomplishment as well as occupy your thoughts.*

Spend time with positive people. *Positive attitudes can be as contagious as negative attitudes. Be with people who support you and lift your spirits.*

Exercise. *If your depression stems from unexpressed anger, physical activity will be especially helpful in dissipating angry feelings from your body and mind.*

Remind yourself that these feelings of depression won't last forever. *Consider how long your previous depression lasted.*

Make the place where you spend the most time pleasing to your senses. *Be sure it is well lit. Fill it with things that remind you of happy experiences and things.*

Concluding The Program

In concluding this program, encourage the youth to try some of the techniques that were suggested during the program the next time they are feeling down. Suggest that they try rating the success of the various techniques so that they might determine which ones work best for them.

IF ONLY.....

Hindsight is 20/20 but unfortunately we don't always have the benefit of being able to see what should have been done in a situation until after it has occurred. Too often we bring ourselves down with thoughts of what we could have done or should have done, if only we had known what was going to happen. We wish we would have been with a friend who needed our help or said "I love you" to a loved one who was killed unexpectedly. It is important for youth to learn to accept that there is nothing they can do about the emotions that the past stirs up, except to try to let them go. As they come to accept that they have no control over the past, they will hopefully learn to let go of the regrets that bring their self-esteem down.

In Preparation

In preparing for this program, contemplate whether you have any regrets from your past that you need to let go of. If so, consider writing down your feelings about it and sharing it with the youth during the program. Then you can tear up and throw away your paper along with the youth at the conclusion of the session.

Opening The Program

Before the program begins, place several kinds of crackers and cookies on a plate along with some pieces of fruit. As the participants arrive, invite them to help themselves to the snacks. After everyone has helped themselves, put away any remaining food. Enjoy some casual conversation as the youth eat their snacks. When everyone is finished, tell them to imagine that, because of circumstances beyond your control, they will be stuck in this room for the next 24 hours. They will receive no more food than that which they have just consumed. As the youth react to this, ask them if they would have handled the situation differently had they known what was going to happen in later moments. Would they have selected more cookies and crackers? Would they have saved some of the snacks to eat later? Point out how it was impossible to know the importance of choosing and eating their snacks wisely without knowing what was going to happen in the next moment.

Continuing The Program

From this conversation, lead into discussion on specific experiences of regretting decisions. The following questions may help in fostering discussion.

❑ *Have you ever had an experience in which the decision or action you made turned out not to be the best choice, given the results?*

❑ *Did you feel responsible for something bad happening, even though it was unintentional?*

❑ *Did you have a difficult time forgiving yourself and letting go of ideas of what you might have done "if only you had known"?*

❑ *Looking back, do you still feel as if you could have prevented the bad experience from happening?*

❑ *Are you being fair to yourself when you blame yourself for things happening over which you really had no control?*

❑ *If one of your friends had a similar experience, would you consider him or her responsible for what happened?*

❑ What might you tell a friend in such a situation to keep him or her from worrying about what is already done?

❑ How do you think hanging onto such negative thoughts impacts the way you feel about yourself?

Now invite the youth to participate in a meditation. Ask them to move into a comfortable position and close their eyes. Help them to relax by focusing their attention on their breathing. Then say: "In your mind, go back to a time when you felt bad about something that happened for which you felt responsible. Remember how you felt, how thoughts of what you should have done filled your mind, and how it affected your thoughts about yourself. (long pause) Now let go of those thoughts and think about the present moment. There is nothing you can do about what has happened in the past. What is done is done. Feel the weight of past concerns lift off you as you begin to live in this moment."

If time permits, pass out paper and pencils and have the youth write about the experience they thought about during the meditation. Encourage them to express how they felt and how it impacted their lives.

Concluding The Program

In closing, say a prayer of thanksgiving to God for giving us the freedom to make our own choices. Remind the participants that although it is important to learn from our past experiences, it is also important to let go of negative thoughts and to be positive about the choices God has allowed us to make for ourselves. Invite them to tear up the papers they have just written and throw them away before leaving as a symbol of freeing themselves of the burden.

A Friend In Need

People respond differently to life's distresses. Some need more support; others need privacy. Because of these differences in people's needs, it is not always easy to know how to help a friend. It is a natural reaction for some people to shy away from a friend in trouble. Out of fear of not saying or doing "the right thing," they may assume that maintaining distance is the wisest choice. To the troubled friend, however, it may simply appear as if he or she is being abandoned.

The goal of this program is to help the youth understand that they don't have to have all the answers, they just have to be willing to listen and empathize with a friend in need. In most cases, the job of a supportive friend is to listen and express concern and, above all, to provide a chance to talk matters out.

In Preparation

In preparation for this program, spend some time reviewing and considering the statements that you will be presenting to the youth in opening the program. Reflect on your own experiences by considering: Have you ever felt unsure how to help a friend in need? Have you ever needed a friend to help you through a difficult time but no one seemed to know what to say or do so they avoided you? Take note of any insights you gain through this reflection that you might share.

Opening The Program

Open the program by asking the youth to indicate whether they agree or disagree with the following eight statements. As you go over them, allow time for the participants to discuss their reasons for agreeing or disagreeing. The youth should also be encouraged to share personal experiences or examples that the statements bring to mind.

❏ *Helping a friend in need does not always have to mean problem solving.*

❏ *What matters most is giving a friend the support he or she wants rather than the support we think will be best.*

❏ *If a friend makes it clear that he/she would prefer to face a problem alone, you should respect that request.*

❏ *When a troubled friend is getting adequate help from others, you should not also try to help because too much interference can make the friend feel that the problem is even worse than he or she thought.*

❏ *You should not try to help a friend who often solicits advice from you but never takes it.*

❏ *You should always help a friend in need, even if you disagree with the friend's actions.*

❏ *It is important to draw a line between being responsive to a friend's needs and taking responsibility for his or her problems.*

❏ *If you are unsure of the "right" thing to say or do for a troubled friend, you are better off leaving the friend alone.*

Continuing The Program

Invite the group to divide into small conversation groups of four persons each and assign one of the following role-play situations to each group. First, have each group discuss the situation they have been assigned and then prepare a role-play of the situation, which they can later present to the whole group. Because different groups will have the same situation to present, their role-play will add to the group insight as to how different persons might react to the same situation.

Role-Play Situation One

Julie has been dating a 25-year-old college graduate for two months behind her parents' back. Her parents recently discovered this and have insisted that Julie stop seeing Ramon. You agree with her parents that she shouldn't be dating someone nine years older than her but you have not yet told her so. Now she is constantly complaining about her parents' demands and keeps telling you about how she is managing to see Ramon anyway. Listening to this makes you feel as if she thinks you approve of what she is doing. You have tried to discreetly avoid her but she hasn't seemed to get the hint.

Role-Play Situation Two

Matt's parents have recently divorced. Matt confided in you about his hurt and confusion during his parents' separation and divorce and your support seemed to help him. Now his father has unexpectedly announced that he is getting married and moving out of state. You know how close Matt and his father have been and how Matt must feel as if he's being abandoned. Matt has remained silent on the topic with you. You are not sure whether he prefers to face the problem alone or if he is merely hesitant about broaching a painful subject. You have made attempts to discuss the subject to no avail.

Role-Play Situation Three

After six months of dating, Omar has suddenly broken up with Karen. Since then, Karen has continued to rehash each moment of their relationship in her struggle to figure out where things went wrong. It is all she talks about during breaks at school and she phones you a couple times each evening to discuss the same. From the beginning you have been supportive but it seems as if she is becoming more, instead of less, upset as the days go by. She hardly eats anymore and she shows no interest in her appearance. You are afraid that Karen needs more help than you yourself can offer.

Allow time for the groups to work out their role-play situation. This may take 20 or 30 minutes. Then invite each group to present their role-play to the whole group. Follow each role-play presentation with group conversation about how the persons involved coped with their situation.

Concluding The Program

In concluding the program, say a prayer of thanks for the gift of friends who can support each other in times of need.

ONE LOVE, TWO FAITHS

In our society of people with vast ethnic and cultural backgrounds, one love plus two religions is becoming a common marriage equation.

The youth in your group will undoubtedly develop relationships with people of all different religions throughout their lives—and this will enrich their experiences. But would they consider marrying someone of a different religion or faith?

As the members of your youth group approach adulthood, they need to be encouraged to contemplate the role religion will play in their marriages. Do they think true love is so strong that it outweighs the importance of religion? Or is a common faith a necessity for a fulfilling marriage?

In Preparation

Search throughout your church membership for people whose spouses are of different religions or faiths than their own. Invite them to come share their experiences to help the youth understand the issues involved. The program will have the most impact if you include a speaker who is married to a Christian of another denomination, one who is married to a non-Christian and one whose spouse is of the same faith. This will give the youth a well-rounded view of the role religion has played in three different marriages. It would also be interesting if at least one speaker could bring his or her spouse so that both perspectives of one interfaith marriage are given.

Opening The Program

Before introducing the program's topic, give the participants paper and pencils and ask them to each list the five most important attributes they are looking for in their future spouse. Collect the completed lists and copy each attribute on a chalkboard, indicating the number of times each attribute appears on the lists. Don't be surprised if religion is the furthest thing from some youth's minds as they contemplate the prospect of marriage. Briefly discuss the traits listed on the chalkboard, mentioning religion (assuming it made the list) last. Encourage participants to explain how they decided if religion should be included on their list of important traits. This should lead the youth to answer the fundamental question "How important should religion be in choosing a marriage partner?"

Continuing The Program

Introduce your guests, who may have developed some other points to bring out from listening to the discussion so far. Allow each of them time to share his or her marriage experience. Have them explain why they married as they did with respect to faith and how it has affected their family lives. Be sure that if the speakers have children, they discuss how they have handled having a different faith than their spouse with respect to their children. Encourage the youth to ask questions.

When the speakers have finished, ask the youth again how important religion is in choosing a lifetime mate. Their viewpoints may have changed from listening to the speakers. Ask them to raise their hands if they would marry someone who was not from their denomination. Discuss why they feel the way they do. Then ask them to raise their hands if they would marry someone who was not a Christian at all. Encourage them to explain their responses.

For Discussion

❑ *Do you think it is possible for a couple to share the same values but not the same beliefs? Which is more important—values or beliefs?*

❑ *Do you think it would be good to expose children to both parents' religions? Would this confuse them or help them understand that not everyone thinks the same but people can get along despite differences?*

❑ *Do you think the Bible requires us to marry only Christians? Study II Corinthians 6:14.*

❑ *"Shun youthful passions and pursue righteousness, faith, love and peace along with those who call on the Lord from a pure heart." (II Timothy 2:22). What does this say to you about choosing a mate?*

❑ *Study I Corinthians 7:12-16. Is this telling you something different than the two Bible passages you just read? Which of the three passages comes closest to expressing what you believe about marrying people of different faiths or religions?*

Concluding The Program

Close the session by encouraging the youth to take home the list of traits they each wrote at the beginning of the program. Suggest that they take time to reflect on it and consider if they would change anything in light of the discussion that took place.

BACK TO THE FUTURE

What images fill your mind when you think about the future? Are your feelings ones of hope and promise or more of fear of the unknown? Ask your youth group these questions and you are likely to get as many different answers as you have participants. But one thing they all share in common is that they think about the future—a lot.

For the younger members of the group, thoughts of the future may not extend much beyond high school. They may think more about what their senior year will be like than what the years beyond that will hold. Older members, on the other hand, should be thinking about life after high school. To give your group a common point for discussion, this youth program asks teens to consider what life will be like ten years after high school graduation. The discussion and activities will get youth considering the lifestyle and future they want and help them outline what they can do now to pave the way.

In Preparation

Prepare for this program by spending some time looking back at the future goals you held for yourself as an adolescent. How many of those goals did you actually pursue and achieve? How did your goals change over time? Did you make all of the decisions about these goals? Who influenced you? Share these insights with the youth during the session.

Opening The Program

Have a wide selection of magazines for the group members to look through as they arrive. Ask each person to select and cut out five pictures illustrating different lifestyles. Have them rank the pictures from the lifestyle they find least desirable to the one they find most desirable. When everyone is finished, invite different individuals to share their pictures and explain why they ranked them the way they did. Conversation should center on their first and last choices. Foster discussion by asking how many people's first choice lifestyle is much like the one they already have. How many people selected first choice lifestyles that were more idealistic—lifestyles they hope to have in the future?

Now that the participants are thinking about how they would like to see themselves living in the future, invite them to take a closer look at the years to come. Pass out paper and pencils. Tell them to imagine that it has been a decade since they graduated from high school and they are preparing to go to their ten year reunion. They have each been asked to write a 200 word description of what they have done since high school for inclusion in a reunion yearbook. Remind them to be sure to include where they live, what they do for a living (occupation), whether they are married, what their educational background is (college, graduate school), if they have children, and how they spend their leisure time.

When the participants are finished with their descriptions, have them consider the following questions:

❑ *Did you find it difficult to map out where you want to be ten years after high school? What were the most difficult aspects to decide or choose?*

❑ *Would you have written your description differently if you were writing it for personal use rather than for review by your peers? Were you thinking of what would sound most impressive to others or were you honestly thinking about what would give you the greatest feeling of accomplishment and satisfaction?*

❑ *How many of your plans are materialistic? How many are spiritual? Do you consider this a good balance?*

❏ *Has your Christian faith affected decisions concerning your lifestyle and occupation? If so, how?*

Continuing The Program

Now that the participants are aware of—and probably overwhelmed by—the possibilities their futures' hold, take some time to remind them that they do have significant impact on the direction their lives may go. Emphasize that while it is impossible to control or even predict the future, they can steer the way if they stay focused on specific goals. The important thing is to have a clear idea of exactly what (or where) they want to be and to develop some understanding of what it takes to get there.

Introduce the following exercise as a way of helping them begin to formulate ideas on what they should be doing to lead the way to the future they want. Give the participants each another piece of paper and ask them to imagine that they could do or become anything in the world they choose by the time they attend their ten year high school reunion. These wish lists may include more goals than their ten year reunion description or it may simply be a paring down of that description to just list specific objects. Ask them to list every possible thing they visualize themselves doing ten years after high school. When this is complete, have them go back and list the gift or talent they believe will be most essential to achieving each goal.

Now have them go to the opposite extreme and narrow down their accomplishments to just one. If they could accomplish only one thing on their lists before their ten year reunion, what would it be? What makes them value this goal so highly? Have them review their lists and see what talent they thought their most valued goal required. Is that one of their strong points? If they pursued the fantasy of their choice, what would be their next step?

❏ *How much of what you are doing in your life now will help you in attaining your goals?*

❏ *What obstacles do you think you will have to contend with in order to get where you want to be by the time of your ten year high school reunion?*

❑ *How do you think your set of goals compares to the one your parents may have for you?*

Concluding The Program

Conclude the program by inviting everyone to write a brief, long-range plan for reaching the goals they want by their ten year high school reunion. Allow those who wish to share their plan with the group.

GIVING THANKS

Thanksgiving offers an opportunity to take time to count our harvest blessings. It should further remind us that real affluence is not material possessions. No one is so poor in our country that they cannot count one of the blessings of health, love, peace or courage.

Yet whether our blessings are few or many, we often fail to express our gratitude. In part this may be because we have come to take our blessings for granted. It may also be because we feel uncomfortable expressing our gratitude to others. This program is aimed at helping the youth to explore the things for which they should be thankful, the ways they currently express their thanks, and ways they might better reflect that gratitude in the future.

In Preparation

In preparation for this program, review the exercises through which you will be leading the youth and try them yourself. Make a list of the things for which you are thankful this Thanksgiving. Consider how you would express your thanks to people if you had only one day left to do so. Spend some time thinking about how you show your gratitude to others. Share these insights with the group during this program.

Opening The Program

Begin the program by giving the youth a chance to take count of their blessings. Give them each a piece of paper and a pencil and invite them to make a list of the blessings for which they can thank God this Thanksgiving. Remind them that this list may include people and objects, as well as such things as freedom or love.

When their lists are completed, ask the youth to imagine that they have one day left to spend with the people on their lists for whom they are thankful. Suggest that they ask themselves for what they thank each person and then try to express that in their final acts of thankfulness. Encourage the youth to spend a few moments in silence imagining the responses they would receive from the people for whom they are thankful in expressing their gratitude.

After everyone has completed this exercise, invite them to share their reactions. Ask some of the following questions to help foster discussion:

❑ *How did you use your one last chance to express your gratitude?*

❑ *Was it possible to show your true thankfulness in just that one day or not? How long would it take to really show your appreciation?*

❑ *Were some people surprised that you were grateful for the help or support they have given you?*

Continuing The Program

Now move the conversation into a more general discussion about expressing thankfulness by asking some of the following questions:

❑ *What things do you almost always express thankfulness for?*

❑ *Are there things you can think of that you almost always fail to feel gratitude for—in other words, take for granted? Have you ever had difficulty saying "thank you" to someone? What made it difficult?*

❑ *Does it become more difficult to express the thanks we feel if we let time pass?*

❑ *Do you ever feel uncomfortable*

accepting a word of thanks from others? Why?

❑ *How do you feel when someone fails to thank you for something you have done for them? Even if you did not make the gesture to* *get recognition, does the lack of a "thank you" make you feel as if your act was unappreciated?*

❑ *Do you ever say thank you to God? How does it make you feel?*

After all the youth who wish have shared their responses to the questions, read I Peter 4:10: "As each has received a gift, employ it for one another." Discuss together what it means to each of the youth. Suggest that another way of showing gratitude is by sharing your gifts with others. Now invite them to use the other side of their blessings list to write down the gifts they are currently sharing with others.

When they are finished, invite those who wish to name some of the special gifts they have to share. Then enlist them in a discussion of ways they can share these gifts to the glory of God this Thanksgiving. Ask the youth to name them or problems or needs they see in the community. Use these in a column on one side of a piece of posterboard or a chalkboard. On the other side, work together to make a list of things the group can do to help.

Allow the youth to choose one project that they would like to work on this Thanksgiving and follow through by making arrangements for this effort.

Concluding The Program

Close with a prayer of thanksgiving asking for God's help in sharing their blessings with others.

75

THE MEANING OF CHRISTMAS

Despite annual vows to "put Christ back in Christmas" Advent continues to be filled with traditions that stem from the Christian celebration as well as the secular holiday. By identifying the way they participate in Advent, youth may be helped to see that they have a choice whether the time will be just a holiday or whether it will take on the dimensions of a holy time. The goal of this program is also to help youth clarify the meaning they may find in past Christmases and help them develop new meanings for future Christmases. It is important that this be a time of raising questions that the youth may ponder for themselves, rather than offering answers.

In Preparation

In preparing for this program, spend some time thinking about what Christmas means to you personally. Lead yourself through the opening exercise of listing Christmas preparations and then categorize them as reflecting either the secular celebration or the Christian celebration. Be sure to list various ways your church prepares for Christmas so these may be added to the list the youth develop.

Opening The Program

You might begin the program by announcing the number of days left until Christmas. Invite youth to share their initial reaction to this statement—is it a feeling of excitement over the celebration or worry over all they have yet to do? Discuss how although Advent is a time of preparation for God's gift of love in the Christ child, the days leading to Christmas often reflect more of the secular holiday than they do the religious one.

Invite the group to name ways they prepare for Christmas with their families (decorating the house, caroling, shopping for gifts, sending out cards, putting up the creche). List these preparations on a sheet of newsprint or a chalkboard. Then invite the youth to share ways they prepare for Christmas in church and school. List these as well. Now, on another sheet of newsprint, put the heading CHRISTIAN CELEBRATION on the left and SECULAR CELEBRATION on the right. Ask the youth to determine which of the preparations they have named are for Christmas as a celebration of Christ's birth and which are for the secular holiday. Then write the various preparations under the appropriate headings. These should be categorized according to the consensus of the group. If an agreement cannot be reached, list the preparation in both categories.

Continuing The Program

By looking at the list of ways your youth prepare for Christmas, you will likely come up with several questions that will foster discussion. Be sure to have them share their reasoning for placing the various preparations in one category over the other. Here are some other questions you might pose:

❑ *Did you have a difficult time trying to separate the secular celebration of Christmas from the Christian one? Why?*

❑ *Which of the preparations listed do you enjoy? Which don't you enjoy? Are they all necessary?*

❑ *Do you believe that gift-giving is a part of the Christian celebration of Christmas?*

❑ *How do you show that Christmas is a religious holiday in your gift-giving?*

❑

❑ What is the most meaningful Christmas gift you have ever given someone? What is the most meaningful gift you have ever received? What made these gifts so special?

❑ What might Christmas be like if gifts were not exchanged?

❑ What does it mean to you to celebrate Jesus' birth?

❑ If Jesus were on earth today to see how you celebrate his birthday, what do you think he would say about it?

❑ What made the happiest Christmas of your life so special?

❑ Have you ever experienced the truth of the statement, "It is better to give than to receive"?

❑ What specific way can you reflect Christ's love to others who are in need?

After the group has thoroughly discussed these questions, there are two ways you might wish to continue the program depending on the time left and the youth's interest. One idea would be to allow the youth to spend time in quiet reflection and then write out their vision of a perfect Christmas. An alternative to this would be to make this a time in which the youth actually put into practice some of the things they have discussed. They might make gift certificates for things they can do for others or plan out a project in which they can help the needy this season.

Concluding The Program

Conclude the program with a prayer seeking help in making the coming of the Christ Day more meaningful for ourselves and others.

EMPHASIS ON EPIPHANY

The weeks following Christmas can often be a letdown after the anticipation and celebration of the Advent season. But the 12 days of Christmas lead into the season of Epiphany which also brings hope and happiness because it celebrates Christ's appearance to all the world. As you prepare youth programs for use during this season—which begins January 6 and lasts until Ash Wednesday—don't overlook how effectively a study of Jesus' appearance to the world and the onset of his ministry will tie into exploration of the events of Lent. Following are five program starters based upon themes related to Epiphany. You might either combine the themes into one program or expand each theme into individual programs.

EPIPHANY

Depending upon how your church has observed Epiphany in the past, it might be beneficial to dedicate a youth program to a review of what this season is all about. Because the Magi are often included as part of the Christmas pageant, there may be some confusion about the arrival of the Magi actually being a separate event as recorded in scriptures. You might begin this program with a reading and discussion of Matthew 2:1-12.

Explain that the themes of Epiphany come from the Greek word *Epiphaneia* which means "to make known" or "to show forth." The reason the Magi are so important is that their coming and worshiping shows that Jesus came for the Jews and the Gentiles. Discuss briefly the three manifestations of Christ's glory that Epiphany celebrates—the adoration of the Magi, his baptism, and his first miracle, the transfiguration of water and wine at Cana.

Given this perspective of the reason for the season, you might invite the youth to share what life experiences they relate to Epiphany.

THE GIVING OF GIFTS

The season of Epiphany is celebrated in the Epiphany story, the story of sharing gifts. Jesus' identity and divinity were revealed through the visit, worship and gifts of the Magi. The gifts the Magi presented to Jesus were symbols of how they felt about him.

It would be interesting to ask youth to write what gifts they would bring if they were Magi coming to the manger today. Relating their gifts to the gifts that the Magi brought, you might suggest that they offer three gifts, one of financial value to represent gold, one useful or practical object to represent frankincense, and one which is a quality such as joy or peace to represent myrrh. Be sure to encourage the youth to explain how each of these gifts reflects the way they feel about Jesus.

From this activity, you might lead into discussion about gifts the youth have that they might share with others. To help them take account of what they have to offer, ask the youth to complete the following statements:

People like me because...

My most unique talent is...

The best thing I ever did was...

The best gift I ever gave was...

It would also be interesting to have each participant list all the names of the persons present and beside each name list one gift they believe that person possesses.

80

BAPTISM

The beginning of Jesus' ministry certainly was his baptism. Therefore the Epiphany season lends itself to an exploration of the meaning and power of baptism.

You might begin discussion with the account of Jesus' baptism in Mark 1:9-11. As a group or in pairs explore the following scriptures and discuss how they pertain to baptism: I Peter 2:9; Hebrews 9:15; Romans 6:3-4; Joel 6:3-4; John 15:16; Romans 5:6; Ezekiel 36:25-26.

Considering the biblical perspective of baptism, pose the following questions:

❑ *Why did Jesus go to be baptized?*

❑ *What happened when Jesus was baptized?*

❑ *Did Jesus command his followers to baptize?*

❑ *Are we instructed in the Bible to participate in the sacrament of baptism?*

Then lead into a more general discussion of baptism. Be sure to describe the three different methods of baptism used in churches and their symbolism. Discuss how baptism is administered in your church. Questions to foster discussion could include:

❑ *Can we be Christians without being baptized?*

❑ *Does being baptized make us Christian?*

❑ *In what way does baptism signify a relationship with God?*

❑ *How do we experience baptism with our senses?*

❑ *In what way does water symbolize what baptism is all about?*

MIRACLES

Jesus' first miracle—the transfiguration of water and wine at the Wedding in Cana—is celebrated during the season of Epiphany. This would be an ideal time to undertake a study of Jesus' miracles.

You might offer the following definition, found in A Handbook of Theological Terms, in leading off discussion:

"Miracle—In the New Testament, certain events are described as 'powerful deeds' (dynameis), 'wonders' (terata), and 'signs' (semeia). They were, as the words suggest, regarded as manifestations of the power of God believed to be uniquely at work in Jesus."

Discuss the definition and then invite the youth to list as many of Jesus' miracles as they can.

In a society where to see is to believe, it is important that you spend some time discussing the youth's perspective on Jesus' miracles and if they have a difficult time believing in them. Read together the account of the Wedding at Cana in John 2:1-11. Ask the youth to imagine what it would have been like for them to have been there. Would it have been easier to believe at the time than it is reading about it now?

It would also be fun to have a youth night wedding celebration in recognition of the significance of the Wedding at Cana. Encourage some of the youth to do research ahead of time so they might try some authentic folk wedding dances.

LIGHT TO THE WORLD

Epiphany is a time to celebrate the fact that Christ came for all of the world. With this in mind, why not have youth learn more about the missions with which your church is involved? Once they have determined the countries where your denomination has missionaries, have them study the cultures there.

Also invite the youth to think about places in their community that could use their help and to which they could bring the light of Christ. Assist them in making specific plans which they can follow through on this week.

Looking Beyond The Packaging

As George Bernard Shaw once said, "The worst sin towards our fellow creatures is not to hate them, but to be indifferent to them; that's the essence of inhumanity." Yet we are often so busy or focused that we overlook the true value of the many people with whom we come in contact. Considering parts of the Christmas story may be a unique way for your youth to examine just how likely they are to judge others by the packaging, rather than the person.

In Preparartion

In preparing for this session, spend some time reflecting on your own experiences with unfair first impressions, both as the person forming one and the person being judged. Consider what friendships you would have cheated yourelf of if you hadn't gotten past the negative impression you first had of the people. Recall how it felt to be judged unfairly. Take note of any insights you might share during the program.

Beginning the Program

Begin the program by telling the participants that you are going to tell them a story without an ending and it will be up to each of them to complete the story in the way they choose. Remind them that although they have heard this story many

83

times over the years, this time it is different. This time they are part of the story with control over how it concludes. Encourage them to relax and listen to the paragraph you are about to read, keeping in mind that it is actually told from their point of view.

I had been running from chore to chore all day trying to keep the many people who filled my inn happy. Finally I was able to sit down and relax as guests began to turn in for the night. After a moment's rest, a knock at the door brought me back to my feet. I was surprised and disheartened to find an ordinary young couple standing there, the woman looking as though she were going to have a baby any moment. I felt a pang in my heart as her frightened husband said the words I was dreading: "I am looking for a room for the night." His wife looked so close to having a baby, but I had given away my last room hours ago...

Pass out paper and pencils to the participants and ask them to write down how this story would have concluded if they had been the innkeeper. Allow them about 10 minutes to spontaneously conclude just that scene of the familiar Christmas story.

When they have finished, invite one participant to share his or her conclusion to the scene. Then invite those who consider their stories to be significantly different from the one shared to read their conclusions. Ask the group to indicate how many managed to find a room for the couple, how many offered an alternative (such as "the stable"), or how many turned the couple away. It is unlikely that any of the youth opted to send the couple away, given all that they already know about this story and the soon-to-be-born Christ child.

Thus, undoubtedly most of these stories will be positive—but are they realistic? Ask the group to consider how their stories would have been different if they hadn't known the true and wondrous purpose of Mary and Joseph's journey. This is a good way to lead into some questions and discussion about first impressions. If today you owned a motel that was filled to capacity and an average man with an expectant wife asked for a room, what would be your first response? Is it possible that you, already tired from a long day yourself, might have been put off by the appearance of this average couple who had traveled such a long and wearing journey? Do you always take the time to look beyond the appearance of others to consider who and what they are inside?

Have the group also consider how the Christmas story might have been different if the Wise Men had not believed that the Son of God would actually begin his earthly life in a stable in an obscure village with an average couple. At the end of their long journey to see the Christ child, they found a baby in a bed of straw, a lowly and common grass. The Wise Men saw something special. They saw Jesus, the Christ. What would have been your first impression?

Share with the group how the Christmas story says a lot about not judging people by their packaging. It is often difficult to simply see someone's worth without first getting to know them. Then discuss:

❑ *Have you ever been judged by others based upon what they saw of you, rather than how you really were inside? How did this make you feel?*

❑ *Have you ever decided what someone was like before you*

ever got a chance to really know them?

❑ *Have you ever been surprised that your first impression of someone was not very accurate? Can you share an example?*

Concluding The Program

Conclude the program by having the participants think of one person they often come in contact with but have never really bothered to get to know. Encourage them to give themselves a Christmas gift this year by giving this person a chance and letting him or her into their lives.

CARING FOR CREATION

The summer seems a natural time to turn our thoughts to ecology and the fullness of the earth as we find more opportunities to be outdoors. Here are outlines for three programs which you might develop into a series for your youth group. Some of the programs outlined center on discussion, others emphasize activities including "fun" exercises —to help keep youth's attention during the less regulated season of summer. Guest speakers and films or videos will also enhance the programs and help you focus on issues that are of particular concern to your community, city or state. The youth, too, will likely have pertinent ideas and information to share as their schools have undoubtedly exposed them to the concerns of our environment.

First Program:

CARING AS CHRISTIANS

To help the youth explore and consider their personal responsibility for God's world and its future.

Questions for Discussion:

- ❑ *Whose responsibility is it to take care of God's world?*

- ❑ *Do Christians have even more motivation than the general public to help stop widespread pollution since we believe that God created the earth and left it in our care?*

- ❑ *In helping people understand the need to care for the earth, the focus is often on the benefits humanity will reap from a healthier earth. As Christians do you think we have a responsibility to go beyond that motivation to stress that the earth should be valued, respected and nurtured simply because it was created by God and gives glory to God?*

- ❑ *Do you agree or disagree that when we harm the earth we show contempt for its Creator?*

Activities:

1 Read and discuss Genesis 1:28-30. This passage says that humans have been given "dominion over the fish of the sea and over the birds of the air and over every living thing that moves upon the earth." Ask: Does this say to you that humans have a responsibility to care for wildlife or that human needs are more important than those of animals? Divide the youth into groups and pose the question: In what instances, if any, do human beings' rights to land outweigh native animals' rights to remain undisturbed? Invite them to devise solutions to situations, such as destruction of rain forests, that accommodate both the needs of people and wildlife.

2 Divide the participants into small groups and tell each group that they are to come up with a description of an ideal world. Together they are to act as creators and decide what things they would leave the same and what things they would change about our present world. After about fifteen minutes, have them return to the large group and share their visions of an ideal world.

Second Program:

A CARING LIFESTYLE

To consider the impact their lifestyles may have on the environment now and in the future.

For more centuries than we can comprehend, the earth has been plowed, mined, depleted and polluted in more ways than we can imagine. We have become accustomed to time-saving, labor-saving, and in some cases, money-saving devices that are a drain on our natural resources or that create problems in their disposal. Yet by God's grace, the earth continues to supply the resources that sustain the lives of people and animals in ever-increasing numbers.

Open the program by sharing these thoughts with the group and then invite them to answer: If humans continue to live the way they do, how long do you think the earth can provide the resources needed and handle the waste produced?

Questions for Discussion:

❑ *How much of an impact do you think your lifestyle has on the environment?*

❑ *Have you changed any of your habits after becoming aware that they had detrimental affects on the environment? Share these and other examples of how the quickest, easiest and most convenient ways of doing things aren't always the best methods in terms of environmental consequences.*

❑ *How would your lifestyle change if your entire family were limited to one car and enough gas to go 200 miles a week? Which uses of the car would you be most willing to sacrifice: to go shopping, to go to school, to go to work, to go to church, to go on dates, to go out with friends?*

❑ *How would your life be affected if your family were required to cut its energy use in half? Which of the following would you be most* willing to do without: stereo, TV, hairdryer, clothes dryer, dishwasher, microwave, air conditioner, central heating system, refrigerator, freezer?

Activities:

1 Divide the participants into two groups. One group is to role-play new arrivals from an imaginary planet. The other group is to be people concerned about the environment. The new arrivals should consider what they would think of the world if seeing it for the first time. What questions would they have? The "environmentalists" should create guidelines for the wise use of resources. What do the newcomers need to know about God and our relationship with God? What rules will help them learn to use resources wisely? They should think of things the new arrivals should do as well as things they shouldn't do.

2 Invite an articulate elderly member of the congregation to talk about life during the Depression. This discussion could revolve around how people then were forced to reduce their buying and reuse many things—essentially change their style of living. Beforehand, have the youth prepare a list of questions they would like the guest to answer.

Third Program

CARING AS A CHURCH

To consider the role that the Church, as well as the local church of which it is a part, should play in caring for the earth.

Questions for Discussion:

❏ *What more should the Church be doing to help preserve the environment and natural resources?*

❏ *Should the Church take a more active role in rejecting policies on the part of some persons and institutions that it believes are damaging the environment or draining natural resources?*

❏ *Do you think it is a responsibility of your church to educate its* members about environmental problems and actions they can take to address them?

❑ What things does your church do to model to its members how to be true stewards of the earth? What other things might it do?

Activities:

1 Invite the minister or another representative from your church to visit the group and discuss what the church is doing to address environmental issues. If your church has a committee dedicated to such issues, have the members from that group come share their purpose and things they are doing to meet their goals. Have the youth develop questions to pose to the guests before they arrive.

2 Have the youth group explore your church to determine how "green" it is. Is recycled paper used in the church office, as well as for bulletins and newsletters? Is there a place for recyclables to be separated in the kitchen and other important places? Are signs posted reminding people to turn off lights when leaving the room? Are bulletins and church school materials recycled? Is ride sharing to church services, meetings and activities organized or encouraged?

3 Have the youth role-play a scenario in which an industry is considering relocating to your town. It would mean many new jobs for people—including members of the church—but a hazardous waste disposal site would have to be set up. Have the participants divide into two groups: those who believe the church should take an active role in opposing the industry and those who support the new industry.

A SERVICE FOR CARING

From the insights that the youth have develped over the course of these programs, have them prepare a worship service to share with the congregation that emphasizes Christian stewardship and reverence for all of life. As a group they should select the Bible reading and hymns that best reflect this reverence. They might also write a prayer of confession for our misuse of the air, sea and earth as well as a litany of thanks for creation.